D1528831

CLASS IN AMERICA

THE FUTURE OF
WORK IN AMERICA

BY DUCHESS HARRIS, JD, PHD

WITH KARI A. CORNELL

Essential Library

An Imprint of Abdo Publishing | abdopublishing.com

ABDOPUBLISHING.COM

Published by Abdo Publishing, a division of ABDO, PO Box 398166, Minneapolis, Minnesota 55439.
Copyright © 2019 by Abdo Consulting Group, Inc. International copyrights reserved in all countries.
No part of this book may be reproduced in any form without written permission from the publisher.
Essential Library™ is a trademark and logo of Abdo Publishing.

Printed in the United States of America, North Mankato, Minnesota
042018
092018

**THIS BOOK CONTAINS
RECYCLED MATERIALS**

Cover Photo: Shutterstock Images
Interior Photos: Shutterstock Images, 1, 5, 8, 41, 52–53, 55, 72, 76–77; Paul Sakuma/AP Images, 10,
34; Jared Wickerham/AP Images, 12; Michael Gordon/Shutterstock Images, 15; North Wind Picture
Archives, 17, 18; AP Images, 21, 28; Everett Collection/Newscom, 24, 26; Ron Case/Hulton Archive/
Getty Images, 31; Hyman/AP Images, 32; Stringer/India/Reuters/Newscom, 37; Minerva Studio/
Shutterstock Images, 42–43; iStockphoto, 45, 50, 59, 78–79, 84, 91, 94–95; Katarzyna Bialasiewicz/
iStockphoto, 46–47; Monkey Business Images/iStockphoto, 57; Dennis Van Tine/Abaca/Sipa USA/
AP Images, 62; Francis Joseph Dean/Deanpicture/Newscom, 64–65; Jacob Lund/Shutterstock
Images, 66; Steve Debenport/iStockphoto, 69; Marcio Jose Sanchez/AP Images, 81; Uladzik Kryhin/
Shutterstock Images, 82–83; David Goldman/AP Images, 86; Ben Margot/AP Images, 89; Christoph
Dernbach/picture-alliance/dpa/AP Images, 93; Peter Bennett/Ambient Images/Newscom, 97; Weng
Xinyang Xinhua News Agency/Newscom, 98

Editor: Claire Vanden Branden
Series Designer: Becky Daum

LIBRARY OF CONGRESS CONTROL NUMBER: 2017961142

PUBLISHER'S CATALOGING-IN-PUBLICATION DATA

Names: Harris, Duchess, author. | Cornell, Kari A., author.
Title: The future of work in America / by Duchess Harris and Kari A. Cornell.
Description: Minneapolis, Minnesota : Abdo Publishing, 2019. | Series: Class in America | Includes
        online resources and index.
Identifiers: ISBN 9781532114083 (lib.bdg.) | ISBN 9781532153914 (ebook)
Subjects: LCSH: Job vacancies--United States--Juvenile literature. | Equal employment
        opportunity--Juvenile literature. | Job hunting--United States--Juvenile literature. | Job
        vacancies--Effect of technological innovations on--Juvenile literature. | Social classes--
        United States--History--Juvenile literature.
Classification: DDC 301.451--dc23

CONTENTS

ONE

THE FUTURE WORLD
OF WORK

magine a typical Monday in 2030. Instead of jumping into your automated car or hopping on public transit to make your way to an office, you begin the day in your kitchen, wearing pajamas and eating breakfast while you scan job postings online. Only you're not sitting in front of a laptop—the "computer" is merely an access screen projected on a wall in your kitchen. When you walk into the room, the computer recognizes your digital identity and automatically logs you in. You operate it by touching and sweeping through menus and screens. In fact, you have many access screens like this in different rooms of your house, all connected to the cloud. Most of the time, though, you simply ask Simon, your computerized, intelligent assistant, to

Working from home is becoming an increasingly popular option for workers in the United States.

find what you're looking for. "Simon, please show me all graphic design jobs available through next month."

The job offerings range from three- to four-week projects to tasks that will take only one day to complete. They are organized into categories, so you scan all jobs that might interest you available through next month. You see a couple of projects that look interesting and appear to match your skill set, so you quickly send off a link to your job profile, a video clip you created highlighting your work experience and showcasing samples of your work. Simon anticipates your next search before you can even ask: "I've brought up the list of handyman and maker's tasks in the area as well." You thank Simon and take a look at the offerings, noticing that a person in your neighborhood just bought a bed from IKEA and needs someone to assemble it. Someone across town is looking for a skilled painter to paint the trim on his or her house. You could do either of these jobs, but you message the neighbor first, because she is close by. Putting together the bed will keep you busy while you wait to hear back on the graphic design gigs, and it will get you out of the house. You hear back from the neighbor right away and the job is yours. You quickly finish eating and run off to begin your day of work.

THE FUTURE IS NOW

This work model, an example of what is called the "gig economy," represents one theory of how the future of work might look in America. Although it seems futuristic, most of what happened on that typical Monday in 2030 is happening in some form today. In the year 2030, the time when American workers left for an office downtown to put in an eight-hour day, five days a week, may be a distant memory. Not only may nine-to-five jobs be a thing of the past, it will likely be quite rare for an employee to work for the same company throughout his or her entire career, as was common in the past.

In a gig economy, freelancers and contract workers piece together an income by seeking out and completing a number of jobs throughout the year. There are even websites, such as Upwork, where workers with a wide variety of careers or skill sets can look for current projects. On other sites, such as TaskRabbit, people can post around-the-house projects they need to have completed. And most people are familiar with Apple's Siri and Amazon's Alexa, two forms of artificial intelligence (AI) known as intelligent assistants that operate like Simon.

WORKING LESS IN THE FUTURE

As AI and automation continue to improve systems and efficiency throughout society, experts believe that humans will eventually enjoy more free time and spend fewer hours working each week. The concept of advancing technology resulting in more leisure time for working Americans isn't new. During the Great Depression (1929–1941), economist John Maynard Keynes predicted that by the year 2030, the average hours worked in a week would shrink to 15, less than half of what full-time employees work now.[1]

Technological advancements are happening at a rate much faster than what experts could have predicted ten or even five years ago. Advancements are being made across many disciplines at once, leading to mind-boggling results. For example, architects and designers are using computer design, 3-D printing, synthetic biology, and materials engineering to develop systems in which our bodies are able to interact with microorganisms, the products we use or consume, or the buildings in which we live. These systems are able to react and adjust to new conditions or even anticipate our needs. One example of this is a structure incorporated into a piece of

Amazon's Echo is a speaker with a built-in voice assistant, Alexa. This is just one of the devices available today with AI technology.

clothing that contains living organisms that scan the skin and repair damaged tissue as needed.

CHANGING THE WAY WE WORK

It's no surprise that such sweeping and swift advances in technology are having a profound effect on the workplace. Since the 1970s, automated robots have threatened to take over the jobs of assembly-line workers in factories. And gradually, they have. First, robots were used to complete the most dangerous jobs on the factory floor, keeping human workers out of harm's way. Then automated arms and other robotic devices were used to complete repetitive tasks that didn't require much thought. Today, as technology advancements march on, manufacturing efficiency, rates of production, and profits

THE FACTORY JOBS THAT REMAIN

There are still some factory jobs available to humans. Factories employ highly skilled workers to ensure the computer programs are running properly and to check and adjust precise machinery periodically throughout the day to make sure the manufactured parts are correct. Unskilled laborers are hired to correctly position parts in a mechanism or do other fine-motor tasks that prove difficult for robots. But it's only a matter of time before the manufacturing jobs available for unskilled workers are in danger of disappearing.

Many manufacturing jobs don't offer the same advancing career path they once did. Unlike in the past, entry-level employees aren't able to simply complete on-site training to move up a level on the pay scale. Typically, many next-level positions could be performed by robots, and to move up to highly skilled positions requires at least two years of higher education.

Robots are especially useful in manufacturing when the job at hand is potentially dangerous to humans.

have skyrocketed. The success of automation means factories will continue to find ways to replace workers with robots. In 2015, there were five million fewer jobs in manufacturing in the United States than there were in 2000, a drop of approximately 30 percent.[2]

Factory automation has displaced an entire segment of the middle- and lower-income workforce, and few new jobs in the same pay range have been created to replace those lost jobs. The area that has seen the most job growth is the service industry, which includes many jobs at minimum wage. In fact, 75 percent of US job growth in 2010 was in jobs that paid less than $15 an hour on average.[3] Service industry jobs include those in food service, automotive services, home maintenance, health care, social services, and the hotel and entertainment industry.

WHAT ABOUT OTHER INDUSTRIES?

Automation is a logical fit for the repetitive nature of jobs in the manufacturing industry. But few people believed automation could work with jobs that require thought and decision-making, creativity, or the warmth and care of a human being. However, AI is showing the potential to complete jobs that have long been considered immune to automation. In fact, experts estimate that AI will replace 17 percent of jobs by 2027.[4]

Advancements in AI demonstrate computers are capable of performing more than only repetitive jobs that require little thought. Jobs that are not necessarily repetitive, but are predictable, can now be done by robots.

WINNING CHESS AND *JEOPARDY!*

Progress made at IBM in a relatively short span of time provides a good example of the advances in the ability and potential of AI technology. In 1997, IBM's Deep Blue computer stunned the world by defeating world chess champion Garry Kasparov in a chess match. Less than 15 years later, in 2011, IBM's Watson supercomputer won a round of the popular quiz show *Jeopardy!*, handily defeating two of the show's best contestants. A game of chess has defined rules and specific parameters, making it a game computers can easily excel at. But *Jeopardy!* draws from seemingly limitless banks of knowledge and trivia with no real patterns to speak of. Watson is currently being trained for health care and banking applications.

Examples include bookkeeping, writing legal briefs, or reading medical scans. Psychology has long been a career thought to be out of the reach of AI technology because the assumption was that people would not want to confess their problems to a computer. But some studies indicate the opposite is true. In a study at the Institute for Creative Technologies in Los Angeles, California, people were found to be more honest and forthright when talking to an artificially intelligent virtual human than they were when talking face-to-face with a human psychologist. The reason for this was that they felt less judged when confessing their worries to a computer.

So what do these disruptions in the way we work and the jobs we do mean for the future of work in America? Will there even be work to be done? In the search for answers, experts have looked to how the workforce has responded and adapted in the wake of technological revolutions throughout history.

DISCUSSION STARTERS

- What are some of the factors that have played a part in the disappearance of middle-class jobs?

- Do you think manufacturing jobs will ever go away completely? Why or why not?

- Would working fewer hours in a typical workweek be a bad thing? Explain your answer.

AUTOMATED
CUSTOMER SERVICE

Many jobs in customer service, retail, and banking have been automated for years and will likely become completely automated in the future. Customer-service call centers are one example. When people call in to a customer service line, they will more than likely listen to a series of prerecorded options that guide them to the specific help topic that addresses their question. Or, callers may request the option of talking to a real person. However, IBM predicts that by 2020, 85 percent of customer service interactions will be performed by AI.[5] Since the first automated teller machines, or ATMs, appeared at banks and stores decades ago, these computers have taken the places of many bank tellers.

Self-service checkout lines in grocery and department stores are another example. Although staff members are on hand to help when registers freeze up, far fewer employees are needed to work checkout lanes. McDonald's, for example, aimed to add 2,500 self-service kiosks to many stores in 2017. However, the company insists that this won't mean layoffs for workers. Instead, the fast-food chain says it will switch existing cashiers to different areas in the restaurant. The company is striving to use the kiosks, which aim to be more accurate and efficient than a human cashier, to work alongside people to make the restaurant better for customers.

A self-order kiosk in a McDonald's restaurant

TWO

EARLY WORK IN THE
UNITED STATES

Long before the United States became an industrial powerhouse, it was an agrarian society rooted in farming and craftsmanship. Small farms dotted the countryside, and farmers grew food and raised animals to provide for their own families.

Those who didn't farm worked out of their homes or in small village shops to make items by hand to sell. Spinners spun cotton into thread, weavers wove the thread into cloth, and seamstresses sewed that cloth into clothing.

Early settlers used horses to help farm crops.

The production of cotton had a profound effect on the US economy in the 1800s. Enslaved Africans were forced to work the cotton fields for hours with little or no pay.

THE FIRST INDUSTRIAL REVOLUTION

Throughout history, humans have sought ways to make everyday tasks easier and more efficient. This is as true today with advances in technology and automation as it was more than two centuries ago. The process of spinning cotton or wool into thread and yarn, the key component of America's first industry, was tedious and time consuming. In 1764, Englishman James Hargreaves invented a tool that would make spinning fiber into thread much easier. His invention, which was later called the spinning jenny, made it possible for one worker to spin several spools of thread at one time. This invention would forever change the way people worked around the world.

With technological advances in the textile industry came huge leaps forward in other areas. The invention of the steam engine in 1712 eventually led to steamships and locomotives, which were needed for moving textiles from factory to market. The success of the textile industry led to the mechanization of the production of many other goods. They could now be made more quickly and cheaply than craftsmen could make them.

Not much later, in the 1780s, another Englishman named Edmund Cartwright invented a power loom for producing vast amounts of cloth at one time. The power looms were big and required lots of space, so factories were built to accommodate them. These textile factories became very successful, spurring what became known as the Industrial Revolution.

Although machines made it easier for more product to be made in a shorter amount of time, humans were still a key component in the textile industry. Enslaved Africans had a huge influence on the economies of both the United States and Britain due to their work in the cotton fields in the American South. Africans continued to work in the cotton fields long after slavery was abolished in 1865.

As more factories were built, workers were hired to operate the looms and spinning jennys. People moved from the countryside to the cities to work in the factories. During the next 50 years, the Industrial Revolution spread throughout Europe and to the United States. By 1900, the United States had become the world's leading industrial nation.

POOR WORKING CONDITIONS AND UNIONS

The manufacturing boom ushered in by the Industrial Revolution introduced a new set of problems for the working class. With no set limits on how many hours to work in a day and no rules about working conditions, factory owners demanded workers toil through shifts spanning 12 to 14 hours, sometimes six days a week.[1] Because they were small and could tuck into cramped spaces, children were often assigned dangerous tasks such as fixing broken machinery or cleaning machinery while it was operating. By the 1880s, workers organized into trade unions, organizations that negotiated for better pay and working conditions for employees. Unions still exist today. They continue to ensure that workers are being treated fairly.

MASS PRODUCTION AND THE FORD MOTOR COMPANY

The introduction of the automobile in America in the early 1900s led Henry Ford to look for a way to produce cars more easily. Ford's goal was to make cars affordable to everyday people. To do this, Ford looked for ways to bring costs down and make the process of building cars more efficient.

This quest led Ford Motor Company, based in Highland Park, Michigan, to develop the first assembly-line production for automobiles. Ford's Model T

During the Great Depression, thousands of people waited in line for job opportunities.

car first rolled off the production line in 1908. By 1927, 15 million Model T's had been sold.[2]

STOCK MARKET CRASH

But on October 29, 1929, the stock market crashed, plunging America into the Great Depression. What had seemed like a booming economy was actually an overinflated market. Overspeculation and investments outpaced the actual production and value of goods.

In the West and the Midwest, drought was taking hold, causing crops to be ruined. This perfect storm of events sent the American economy into a tailspin. Consumer spending

GREAT RECESSION OF 2008

In recent history, financial markets took a dive that has been compared with the stock market crash of 1929 and the subsequent Great Depression. According to former head of the Federal Reserve Ben Bernanke, "September and October of 2008 was the worst financial crisis in global history, including the Great Depression."[5] Although the 10 percent unemployment rate wasn't close to the 25 percent during the Great Depression, the near-total collapse of the banking system in 2008 was unlike anything experienced in the past. The recession was in large part caused by mortgage lenders granting home loans to buyers who could not afford the monthly payments. In 2006, when home values dropped throughout the nation, banks granting these mortgages revealed that they had fewer assets than they had claimed.[6] This caused a ripple effect throughout the financial industry. The Great Recession pushed struggling companies to find ways to cut costs. They laid off workers, sent jobs overseas where labor was cheaper, and automated factories. This disruption in the economy has left the future of work in the United States in question.

plummeted. Manufacturing companies stopped churning out goods and laid off workers. By 1932, approximately 15 million Americans were out of work and one-half of the nation's banks had failed.[3]

Unemployment levels in some parts of the country were sky high. In Toledo, Ohio, in 1933, unemployment levels were 80 percent. Things were even worse in Lowell, Massachusetts, the heart of the American textile industry, where the unemployment rate was an overwhelming 90 percent.[4]

PUTTING AMERICANS BACK TO WORK

President Franklin D. Roosevelt took office in March 1933. Within his first 100 days in office, President Roosevelt ushered in several new social reforms and programs designed to boost the US economy and put Americans back to work. Collectively, these reforms were known as the New Deal. After stabilizing the banks and reassuring the American people, President Roosevelt established government programs designed to rebuild the nation's infrastructure.

A key component to President Roosevelt's plan to revive the economy was the Civilian Conservation Corps (CCC). The CCC was a work relief program aimed to employ people in jobs related to the nation's natural resources. By 1933, 300,000 men were hired to put out forest fires, plant trees, and take preventative measures against soil erosion.[7] A few years later, Roosevelt established the Works Progress Administration (WPA), which put three million Americans back to work, building highways, schools, playgrounds, hospitals, and airports. The WPA also funded the work of writers, photographers, artists, musicians, and theater directors.

SOCIAL SECURITY

In addition to work programs, President Roosevelt established a number of safety nets to ensure that working-class Americans would not go hungry if they were to lose their jobs in the future. The Social Security Act, which Congress passed in 1935, provided American workers with unemployment, disability, and retirement pensions. This program, although important, excluded domestic and farm workers. These groups represented 50 percent of the

The Social Security Act was signed on August 14, 1935, by President Franklin D. Roosevelt. Some experts expect Social Security to run out of money by 2035.

workforce at the time, and the majority of these excluded people were black. These two employment groups were added later.

Through the Social Security program, a small percentage of each paycheck is taken out and put toward Social Security. Upon retirement—which was originally set at the age of 65—or in the event that the employee is no longer able to work, the government will issue a monthly check from the Social Security fund. These safety nets are crucial for retired or unemployed Americans and will continue to be in the future.

But just how long it will remain part of the future has been a topic of debate. The main issue is that people are living much longer than they did in the 1930s. Increased life expectancy means that retirees are drawing from Social Security benefits for a longer period before they die. As the population continues to age and there are fewer younger people of active working age, Social Security funds might not be able to keep pace with the benefits being paid out.

AN END TO THE GREAT DEPRESSION

President Roosevelt's New Deal programs improved the economy somewhat and provided a degree of relief to the poor. But it would take the United States' entrance into World War II (1939–1945) to completely lift the nation out of the Great Depression. After the Japanese bombed Pearl Harbor, Hawaii, on December 7, 1941, the United States declared war on Japan and Germany, officially entering the war.

As America's factories tooled up to begin producing ammunition, food rations, warplanes, and battleships, manufacturing companies employed workers around the clock, seven days a week. Those who didn't go overseas to fight in the war were able to find jobs easily, and unemployment dropped to 1.2 percent.[8] Even millions of women, who were previously not a part of the American workforce, found jobs easily during the war years.

The share of women in the US workforce increased by 10 percent between 1940 and 1945.

POSTWAR ECONOMIC BOOM

The United States' gross national product skyrocketed during the war, increasing from $92 billion in 1939 to $220 billion in 1944.[9] On a personal level, the American worker also benefitted during the war years, and incomes rose across the country.

By early 1945, factories had begun to scale down wartime production and convert back to manufacturing civilian goods. Once again, American factories churned out cars, vacuum cleaners, and washing machines. Fears that an economic recession would return when wartime manufacturing ended quickly dissipated. Instead, the US economy continued to grow.

Returning servicemen and servicewomen fueled that growth as they arrived back in the United States eager to settle down and start families. With the help of low-interest loans

WARTIME TECHNOLOGICAL ADVANCES

With the influx of money poured into research and technological advancements during World War II, great strides were made in aerospace and scientific innovations. Two major innovations were the B-29 bomber and the Manhattan Project. The B-29 bomber was a huge, heavy bomber that flew at high altitudes. The Manhattan Project led to the development of the atomic bomb. In the closing weeks of the war, B-29s dropped atomic bombs on Japanese cities. The accomplishment of both these monumental projects ultimately won the war. Each required a massive commitment of capital and resources, as well as a highly organized network of laboratories and manufacturing centers. These technological breakthroughs translated into US economic growth and innovation after the war.

Workers in this factory went from creating materials for war to building washing machines in 1945.

offered through the GI Bill, many newlyweds bought homes in new suburban neighborhoods—a dream that was unattainable for most before the war. And these young families began having children. In 1946, 3.4 million babies were born in the United States, a record-breaking increase of 20 percent from the year before.[10] This was the beginning of the "baby boom," which would span the 1940s through the mid-1960s.

Returning veterans went back to work with bright prospects in an era of prosperity. Boosted by the wartime economic boom, many incomes doubled within a generation, lifting millions of office and factory workers into the middle class. Unionized factory jobs paid well and served as stepping-stones to the middle class. Even blue-collar workers were able to afford luxury goods such as TVs and cars for the first time. With this increase in income, American families had a better standard of living than their parents' generation. By the early 1970s, the United States was one of the leading countries in the world in disposable income.

The growth that has occurred throughout US history has shaped and molded the workforce of America today. Technology changed the world of work, just as it continues to do today. Social Security, which came as a response to the Great Depression, remains a vital part of American workers' lives. The history of work in America has greatly impacted the country and will continue to be an influence in the future.

DISCUSSION STARTERS

- How did the Industrial Revolution change the way people lived?

- How do you think President Franklin D. Roosevelt's New Deal program has shaped the workforce of America today?

- Do you think that Social Security will disappear by the time you retire? Why or why not?

THREE

TECHNOLOGY AND
GLOBALIZATION

As American workers enjoyed higher incomes and a better standard of living than their parents, business owners were looking for ways to increase profits and lower costs. Harnessing the technological advances made during the war, companies worked on improving the quality of manufactured goods and sought ways to conduct business more efficiently.

THE COMPUTER ANSWERS THE CALL

Developments in early computers during the 1950s paved the way for greater efficiency in many industries, including on the

Robots have been used to help research other technologies for many years. This robot from 1959, which could shave a person's face, was also used to research nuclear energy.

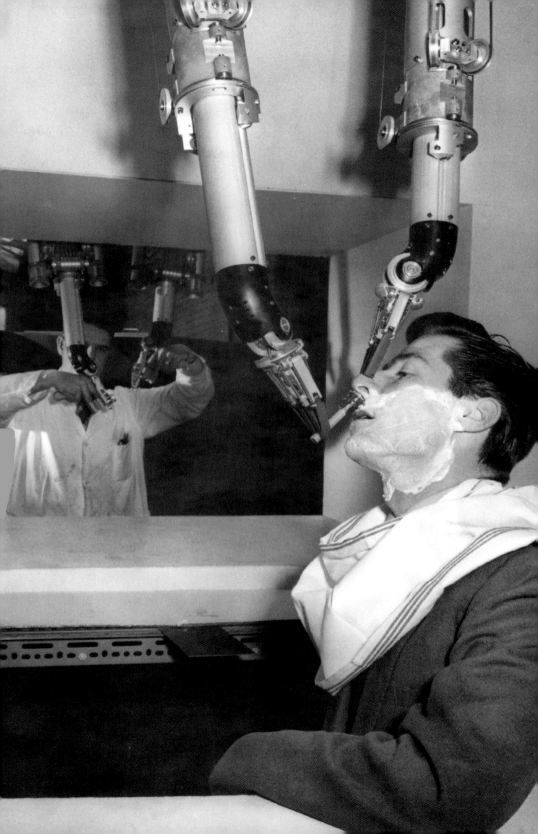

A teen plays on a computer in 1980.

factory floor. As early as 1962, General Motors became the first major company to use an industrial robot, UNIMATE, in its New Jersey manufacturing plant. In 1973, industrial robots developed by ABB Robotics and KUKA Robotics were becoming commonplace in European factories, and US companies followed suit, adopting robots for use in simple assembly-line work.

Improvements in robotic technology were made with each new generation. By 1980, industrial robots controlled by microprocessors were being manufactured in mass quantities, with one new robot hitting the market each month. Yet factory jobs in the United States remained relatively stable, with only dangerous and unsafe jobs falling into the hands of industrial robots.

THE PERSONAL COMPUTER AND THE WORLD WIDE WEB

Advances were being made in other areas of computing as well. On March 12, 1981, IBM introduced one of the world's first personal computers, the IBM personal computer (PC), ushering in the computer age and changing the way people around the world worked. With the help of a PC, letters, books, and other texts could be saved, corrected, updated, and printed without having to retype or use correction tape. Bookkeepers could use computers to calculate sums, create spreadsheets, and do other tasks quickly and easily.

In the decades that have passed since the introduction of the PC, technological advances in computing have accelerated at a more rapid pace than anyone could have predicted. Computers have grown increasingly smaller and more efficient, yet their capacity to store data has expanded considerably. In the early

DRONES IN THE WAREHOUSE

In warehouses throughout the country, automated flying drones are scanning inventory with nearly 100 percent accuracy. In other warehouses, robots are retrieving ordered items from inventory shelves and delivering them to human workers for packing. This is the future of warehouse operations. Not only are the robots and drones accurate, they are efficient. It takes only two automated drones to complete the work of 100 employees in the same time frame. In many warehouses, robots and drones are operating 24 hours a day, seven days a week.[1] Many Americans who once relied on factories for work are losing their jobs to these drones, and it will only become worse in the future.

Steve Jobs, the CEO of Apple, introduced the company's innovative smartphone, the iPhone, in January 2007.

1990s, when the World Wide Web first became available to the public, personal computers became the portals through which users could search databases around the world. The World Wide Web, one of the key parts of the internet, has also become a place where companies can sell their products and conduct business, where people can communicate, and where friends can socialize and reconnect.

The introduction of the iPhone in 2007 meant computers were now small enough to fit into a pocket. The iPhone led to a revolution in the cell phone industry and had a drastic impact on society. Phones soon became cameras, email devices, and internet browsers. Users could also access computer assistants, such as Siri. With these advancements happening at breakneck speed, it has become easier than ever to connect with anyone, anywhere in the world.

This phenomenon had a huge effect on the workforce of America. Employers began to require a set of high-level skills from employees who understood how to use these new technologies. Social media sites, such as Facebook, Twitter, and Instagram, have become platforms on which companies rely to conduct business. Workers in this age need to be digitally literate, understanding how to use the internet, social media, and other digital tools.

These advancements had a positive influence on the economy. In 2015, the internet accounted for 6 percent of the US economy.[2] Not only did the internet make it easier for consumers to access goods, therefore increasing spending, but tech companies also began to hire huge numbers of people. Apple, for example, is responsible for two million jobs across the country.[3] This includes more than the people who work directly for Apple. The company also creates jobs for retailers, app developers, and the suppliers of parts for the devices.

TO OUTSOURCE OR NOT?

It doesn't always pay to outsource. There are plenty of instances in which companies make the decision to keep the manufacturing of more intricate parts in the United States because the highly skilled workforce can be relied on to do quality work. Other times, the high costs of shipping parts made overseas negates any advantages gained by having a lower-cost workforce complete the job. Manufacturers are constantly crunching the numbers and weighing the advantages and disadvantages of outsourcing jobs. Sometimes, it simply doesn't make sense.

GLOBALIZATION AND OUTSOURCING

The giant leaps in communication technology have made it possible for people around the world to interact and do business with the touch of a button. This includes US companies that looked beyond their country's borders in a never-ending quest to find ways to cut budgets and increase profits. Overseas markets where labor and resources are less expensive provided the answer.

In the early 2000s, many US companies began to outsource easy manufacturing jobs to countries with a much lower standard of living, where they could hire more workers at a fraction of the cost it would have been to hire workers in the United States. Globalization and trade agreements gave US consumers access to goods that could be made more cheaply in other countries—sometimes by as much as 80 percent.[4] Another benefit of moving manufacturing operations to other countries is that corporations benefit from fewer regulations, such as safety

Many jobs are outsourced to India because many people there speak English, making it easy for them to communicate with US companies.

requirements for workers and environmental protection rules. They also often pay less in taxes.

In many respects, global outsourcing has had a negative effect on the US workforce. With manufacturing moving overseas, plants at home were shuttered, putting large portions of communities out of work. As steel mills and other factories began to close across the country in the late 1970s through the 1980s, it represented the end of an era for the American worker. For nearly a century, factories had employed workers from a variety of backgrounds and skill levels, leading to an expansion of the middle class. Now, many of those jobs have disappeared, leaving few employment options that offer decent wages. This has had a large effect on communities and society as a whole. When millions of people are put out of work, it in turn brings pain to the community where those people come from.

Americans may continue to lose jobs in the future if companies continue to outsource their jobs internationally. In October 2017, President Donald Trump announced plans to give economic incentives to American companies if they keep their jobs and manufacturing plants in the country. Reversing the process of outsourcing could provide many Americans with jobs. Whether companies will decide to do so is still unknown, however.

ROBOTIC SURGERY

Automation is certainly not limited to factories—robots have even made their way to the operating room. Robots do not replace human surgeons, instead working alongside their human partners to make the work more precise, more accurate, and less invasive. The da Vinci Si is a surgical robot that is composed of three separate robotic arms. The arms are equipped with miniature surgical instruments that are guided with the help of a 3-D camera. The surgeon operates the robotic arms from a control panel in the operating room. The 3-D camera allows the surgeon to see inside the patient during the operation, greatly improving the ability to see the surgical site. Surgeries done by robot have led to fewer instances of infection, less pain, and quicker recovery times. The future of medicine will most likely feature many situations in which doctors and robots are working together.

ROBOTS BUILDING ROBOTS

There is clearly no turning back from increased automation in the current and future global economy. Automation in US factories has accelerated greatly since the Great Recession in 2008. Although the United States has outsourced a significant portion of its manufacturing, China, Japan, Korea, and some European countries have invested in automating their factories and building industrial robots of their own. By not embracing automation in its own factories, the United States could be at a disadvantage. If the country does not step up in building automation, it could fall seriously behind other countries in the world. As jobs are continuing to go in the direction of automation, the United States could become unproductive and inefficient while the rest of the world continues to grow. Many automation experts argue that the United States should dedicate more resources to improving automation and AI technologies.

"We have the opportunity to do something meaningful about reshoring manufacturing," explained Matt Rendall, roboticist and chief executive officer (CEO) at Otto Motors. "The jobs that come back to the US are really only going to work if there's automation involved. But when the jobs come back, and there's robots building the products we consume, will it be an American robot building the product?"[5] This is the question that remains to be answered.

DISCUSSION STARTERS

- Why is automation appealing to manufacturing companies?
- Do you think US-based companies should keep their factories in the United States? Why or why not?
- What predictions can you make about the future of the US workforce as automation becomes more prevalent?

FOUR

THE RISE OF THE SERVICE
INDUSTRY

E ven as manufacturing jobs have continued disappearing, dropping from almost 18 million jobs in 1990 to slightly more than 12 million in 2014, the demand for workers to fill positions in the service industry has been on the rise.[1] As Rob Atkinson, president of the Information Technology and Innovation Foundation, explained, "Most of the savings [from automation] would flow back to consumers in the form of lower prices. Consumers would then use the savings to buy things (e.g., go out to dinner, buy books, go on travel). This economic activity stimulates demand that other companies (e.g., restaurants, book stores, and hotels) respond to by hiring more workers."[2]

In the mid-1990s, jobs in retail stepped in to replace those lost manufacturing jobs. By 2003, the retail industry employed

Restaurant jobs grew faster than jobs in health care, construction, and manufacturing in 2017.

Car dealerships and manufacturers struggled to find enough qualified mechanics and technicians in 2017.

more people than any other industry in 21 states.[3] But the recession of 2008 and 2009 dealt a heavy blow to retail, forcing many shops to close or downsize. Again, jobs were lost, but this set into motion yet another major shift in US employment—the rapid increase of the number of jobs in the health-care industry. Since 1990, the health-care industry has almost doubled in size, jumping from 9.1 million jobs then to more than 18 million in 2014.[4] The implications of this shift in the types of jobs available will have a profound effect on the future of work in the United States.

THE SERVICE INDUSTRY, DEFINED

The service industry encompasses any job that provides a service. Service industry jobs span a wide range of careers, including

high-paying positions, minimum wage jobs, and everything in between.

Service industry jobs can be broken down into the following categories: lodging, personal services, business services, automotive and repair services, legal services, health care, and social services. Lodging includes everything from small motels to luxury hotels. Personal services include things like dry cleaning, tax prep, and hair cutting. Business services include such things as temp agencies and software development. Automotive and repair services include jobs like mechanic and plumber. Social services include things such as day care, older adult care, or private education. No matter what happens to the economy, there will always be a need for services in some shape or form. This need keeps car mechanics, home maintenance

IMPROVEMENTS IN WORK CULTURE

Some companies have worked to make lower-wage jobs more appealing by adding other incentives. Whole Foods, for example, groups workers into teams and gives them a great deal of latitude in how they go about completing their work. The range of freedom among employees gives them a sense of having a degree of control in their work, leading to more job satisfaction. Best Buy gives employees a say in how things are done by encouraging workers to make suggestions for how to improve work processes. Trader Joe's sets the pay scale so that those working full time earn the local median income. The West Coast–based grocery chain is also known for promoting talent from within. Some economists believe this treatment of employees in turn benefits how the company does overall.

In 2018, the hotel industry is expected to grow for the ninth year in a row. This is a trend that hasn't happened since the 1990s, according to a study done by United States Commercial Real Estate Services.

workers, hair stylists, and bookkeepers employed. And, as the baby boom generation ages, one of the most in-demand services will continue to be health care.

HEALTH CARE

Much of the growth in the health-care industry can be attributed to the increasing medical and care needs of the aging baby boom generation. As boomers enter their sixties and seventies and more require supervised care, the demand for nurses in

homes and assisted living facilities is increasing. Other jobs expected to continue to experience growth include physical therapy assistant, nurse practitioner, occupational therapist, physical therapist, and physician assistant.

One of the fastest-growing jobs in the health-care sector is home health aide, and that growth is expected to continue. From 2016 to 2026, the number of home health aide jobs is predicted to increase by 41 percent.[5] The job consists of traveling from one patient's home to another and checking to make sure they have everything they need. This includes some housekeeping, making patients meals, confirming that they've taken any medications they might be on, keeping them company, and reminding them of upcoming doctor appointments.

Home health aides make around $15 per hour, a little less than a decent-paying job in manufacturing would have paid. But the status of the health-care industry, which relies on funding from taxpayers and insurance premiums, is prone to fluctuation. As of early 2018, legislators were considering a major overhaul of the current health-care system, which could affect jobs in the health-care field.

WORKING FOR LESS

Not all jobs are created equal. Replacing manufacturing or warehouse jobs with jobs in the service industry is often a step down in pay for employees. Although some service industry jobs pay well, the majority of service industry work is on the low end of the pay scale. Yet this is where the economy is heading.

Talk of an increase in the minimum wage could entice more full-time workers to remain in service industry jobs, knowing that they have the potential to make a middle-class living. Although the federal minimum wage is $7.25 an hour, states can establish their own higher minimum wages.

In December of 2017 and January of 2018, 18 states had raises in their minimum wages.[6] In New York, the minimum wage bumped up from $10.75 an hour to $11.75 an hour. By 2021, the minimum wage in the state is expected to hit $15. Businesses in Seattle, Washington, that have more than 500 employees and don't offer medical benefits will see a minimum wage of

$15.45 an hour in 2018.[7] But an increase in minimum wage is controversial among business owners because it can mean a significant increase in their payroll, which, in turn, cuts into their profits.

PIECING IT TOGETHER

An increase in the minimum wage would certainly help many service workers, but it doesn't solve other problems inherent in the industry. In many of the low-paying service industry jobs, companies offer only part-time work to keep costs down. If employees work fewer than 40 hours per week, employers don't have to provide health insurance and other benefits, which saves companies a lot of money.

For many working-class families, this means they are working paycheck to paycheck and crossing their fingers that nobody gets sick. As part-time

THE FUTURE OF THE TRUCKING INDUSTRY

One very common service industry job in danger of disappearing with technological advances is truck driver. In 2017, there were 3.5 million truckers crossing America hauling loads of goods.[8] This job, which offers plenty of opportunity for work and pays a decent wage, has been a go-to career for men who didn't go on to college. But autonomous vehicles may soon make this popular profession obsolete. Autonomous trucks have advantages over human drivers. They can be programmed to complete a designated route in a given time frame, they don't need to stop and rest, and they don't get distracted as humans are prone to do, which can lead to accidents. For now, many workers are relying on the hope that companies will value employing Americans over saving money.

workers, most do not receive pay for sick time or vacations, so if a child is ill and needs to stay home from school, the working parent is forced to give up a day of pay to care for the child.

On average, working part-time doesn't provide much disposable income, especially after rent or house payments are made. Therefore, many in the service industry are forced to find other work, sometimes piecing together two or three jobs to make ends meet or get ahead. Some economic experts predict that this trend—working multiple jobs to earn enough money to live on—could very well be the wave of the future.

DISCUSSION STARTERS

- Do you think the service industry will continue to grow? Why or why not?

- Do you think the federal government should increase the minimum wage for all states? Explain your answer.

- What can employers do to make jobs in the service industry more appealing?

FIVE

THE GIG
ECONOMY

nyone who has stayed at an Airbnb while on vacation or nabbed a ride through Uber or Lyft car services has experienced the gig economy firsthand. All three of these companies, which emerged into the marketplace in the past decade or so, provide a digital platform through which individual entrepreneurs around the world may run a business. In the case of Airbnb, people rent out space in their homes, whereas those who work for Uber or Lyft provide rides in their cars. All of these workers are active participants in the gig economy.

Many Airbnb renters and Uber or Lyft drivers have other jobs as well. Two-thirds

Many people enjoy working for Uber because it is a flexible job and drivers can set their own hours.

FOUNDING OF AN AIR BED AND BREAKFAST

In late 2007, when a design conference held in San Francisco, California, led to a shortage of available hotels, Brian Chesky and Joe Gebbia had an idea. Why not add an air mattress to their San Francisco apartment, provide breakfast, and rent space to designers who needed a place to stay? They could make a little extra money to cover the high cost of rent. This idea led to the founding of Airbnb in 2008, a worldwide company that is worth $25 billion today.[3] Through the platform provided by Airbnb, entrepreneurs have been able to make money renting out extra space in their homes or apartments.

of Lyft drivers, for example, drive fewer than 15 hours per week.[1] A worker might begin to rent a room or upstairs apartment on the weekends through Airbnb to earn extra cash. Or a stay-at-home mom or dad may begin to drive for Uber because it's a flexible way to work a few hours while kids are at school. This is the basic concept of a gig economy—piecing together several jobs, tasks, or "gigs" to make a living. And this gig lifestyle is on the rise. According to the Bureau of Labor Statistics, workers who are considered "temporary help" have increased by 50 percent since 2010.[2]

HOW DOES IT WORK?

The gig economy includes freelancing, self-employment, part-time jobs, consulting, contract work, temp work, jobs on the side, and work found or promoted through sites like TaskRabbit or Upwork. The gig economy can exist through digital platforms, such as those provided by Airbnb, Uber, or Lyft. In each of these

In 2016, the average cost of staying in an Airbnb in the United States ranged from $89 to $286 a night.

models, the company provides the website, brand recognition, advertising, and a few ground rules. The individual entrepreneurs cover the cost of the home, car, insurance, or any other liability.

Airbnb and other digital-platform companies take a percentage of what hosts or drivers make to cover operating costs, such as upkeep of the website. But because Airbnb doesn't own the homes and because the individual hosts are not true employees (who would require health care, paid time off, and other benefits), the cost of running this type of business is relatively low.

In addition to covering costs of the home or car, individual hosts and drivers are responsible for communicating with clients, maintaining a schedule, and running any other facets of the business. Hosts can pull their homes off the Airbnb website at any time if they want a break. Uber drivers can do the same, basically setting their own hours and working when they want. This model offers the individual hosts and drivers a great deal of flexibility.

HEALTH CARE, DISABILITY, AND RETIREMENT IN THE GIG ECONOMY

There are many positive aspects to the gig economy. It's flexible, allowing workers to set their own schedules, ramp up hours when they have extra time, and cut back when life gets busy. The gig economy also provides a way for workers to pursue hobbies they've always wanted to dedicate more time to but couldn't

Approximately 25 percent of millennials avoid going to the doctor because of the high costs.

pursue with a full-time job. Some workers may even make a little (or a lot of) money through these hobbies.

But for some workers, the negative aspects of the gig economy far outweigh the positives. As things currently stand, the gig economy offers no safety net to workers. A safety net includes all those perks currently provided by employers to those with traditional full-time jobs—health insurance, paid time off, a retirement plan, and disability insurance or life insurance. By law, companies are required to pay federal and state unemployment taxes, Social Security taxes, federal income taxes, Medicare taxes, and disability insurance for each full-time employee.

And although companies are not required to do so, the employer also typically pays a percentage of each employee's health insurance, disability, and life insurance and makes contributions to employee retirement plans. Large corporations are able to offer benefits to employees at a discounted rate because they are buying multiple policies. Some of the cost of each of these benefits is taken from the employees' paychecks.

People working in the gig economy don't have the benefits of this safety net unless they are covered under a spouse or partner's plan. They can, of course, purchase coverage for health insurance, disability insurance, and life insurance on the open market. But the cost is typically much higher than the amount full-time employees pay because those in the gig economy are paying for the entire cost of their policies.

In addition to covering the cost of safety net expenses, contract, freelance, and other gig workers end up with less

GIGGING THE OLD-FASHIONED WAY

The gig economy doesn't always have to operate through a digital platform. Those in the gig economy also can take a much more grassroots and traditional approach, such as posting a notice in a local coffee shop about housecleaning services or learning about a writing gig from a former coworker. But studies have indicated that workers usually earn more per hour through jobs found on digital platforms than those found by traditional means.

take-home pay than full-time employees. This is because independent workers must pay all of their self-employment taxes, including those for Social Security and Medicare.

This puts workers in the gig economy in a precarious position. As Virginia senator Mark Warner explained, "So these workers, even though they are doing very well, exist on a high wire, with no safety net beneath them. That may work for many of them—until the day that it doesn't. That's also the day that taxpayers could be handed the bill, which is why Washington needs to start asking some tough policy questions."[5]

According to Pew Research Center, 50 percent of adults ages 18–25 were living at home with their parents in 2014. This trend continues to be on the rise as young adults struggle with a challenging job market.

LOOKING FOR SOLUTIONS

One solution that experts advise to people of the gig economy generation is to start saving as early as possible. Although millennials and later generations may not be able to count on Social Security, they can still count on their own savings. According to *Time*, "Saving now is [young people's] surest safety net—and young people have a head start in this category. Compound growth over an extra 10 years may double your nest egg at age 70."[6]

Although that might help for money after retirement, people in the gig economy still worry about how to have money for health care and other benefits. One solution is to create a universal safety net that would work for anyone. Some entrepreneurs participating in the gig economy have taken on the task of devising a plan for portable benefits—personal benefits accounts for workers that they would have access to no matter where they worked.

In an October 2015 letter to Congress, the group of entrepreneurs proposed a portable benefits package, defined by four key points.

FLEXICURITY

In Nordic countries such as Denmark, the government offers flexicurity, a form of flexible Social Security to workers. The program provides support in the form of payments and job training for workers who find themselves between work gigs. Payments are generous, but time spent between jobs is short. The Danish government makes a promise to Danes that if they are laid off, they will find new jobs quickly.

One, benefits would need to be independent, meaning they would not be tied to employment with a certain company. With an independent benefits package, workers would be able to access them no matter where they worked or whom they worked for. Two, the benefits would need to be portable, allowing workers to take benefits with them from one job to the next. Three, benefits should be universal, giving all workers equal access to a standard benefits package, whether or not the worker is currently employed. And four, the approach should be supportive of innovation, meaning businesses should be able to try on different benefits offerings whether a worker is a full-time employee, a part-time contractor, or anything in between.

WHO PAYS FOR IT?

Although these principles provide a solid foundation on which to build portable benefits for gig workers, one big question remains: Who will pay for these benefits? Some have suggested the idea of providing all those of working age with a universal basic income in the form of a monthly payment to each worker from the federal government. The government would raise money for such a program by aggressively taxing the wealthy, a proposal that is controversial among the rich but has garnered support among Democrats and Republicans in the past.

This idea is a familiar one in Europe, where a handful of countries have examined the idea of a basic income to support those displaced by automation and other factors. In Finland,

the government is considering a plan to provide a basic income to everyone, whether they work or not. In a country with a 10 percent unemployment rate, four of five Finns support the concept of a basic income.[7] And in Utrecht, Netherlands, a pilot program that provides a basic income to those who live within the city was underway in January 2017. Perhaps a program along these lines could provide a solution to the safety net issue in the future.

DISCUSSION STARTERS

- If given the option, would you rather be a full-time worker or a worker within the gig economy? Explain your answer.

- Can you think of one way to provide a security net to those who work in the gig economy?

- Do you think the government should pay everyone a basic income? Why or why not?

WORKFORCE
TRENDS

t's clear that the workforce of the future will be one of transition. The rise of the gig economy signals that more workers will earn a living completing many tasks and jobs. And the traditional, full-time work model still common today will become increasingly rare.

This trend has been accelerated by an increase in the number of jobs lost to automation. But it is also gaining momentum as a result of the needs and working styles of the workers themselves. Those workers encompass a wide range of skills and approaches to workplace culture, including millennials on the young end of the workforce spectrum and retiring baby boomers on the other end.

More companies are looking to hire part-time workers.

now hiring

Are you a creative trendsetter with an eagerness to start your career in a fun, fast-paced work environment? If so, we have opportunities for you! Submit your application today or speak with a Manager to learn more!

T·J·maxx®

Millennials are the largest group in the United States' workforce today.

RISE OF MILLENNIALS

By 2020, millennials will make up 35 percent of the global workforce, so this generation's approach to work promises to shape the future.[1] Millennials are a large and diverse generation. Experts define it as those born between 1982 and 2004.[2] Due to the rapid and vast technological advances that occurred during that time frame, millennials in their thirties are drastically different from the teens at the younger end of this range. However, all millennials have at least one thing in common: the workforce that their parents knew is immensely different from the one they will enter.

Having come of age during the Great Recession of 2008, the millennials' approach to work has been influenced by a shaky economy. The first of the millennial generation were graduating college and entering the workforce at the height of the recession. This was a discouraging and overwhelming time as businesses were implementing hiring freezes and offering less-than-stellar salaries. In response, millennials were forced to find part-time jobs, which barely provided enough money to pay off massive college loans, let alone have enough left over to live on. In fact, Forbes magazine notes, "with fewer full-time opportunities, many young workers have resorted to finding gig work to make ends meet—and those small, part-time jobs are oftentimes insufficient to provide anything beyond basic needs and student debt payments."[3]

JOB SECURITY, MILLENNIAL STYLE

Although millennials place a high value on job security, they have a different way of defining it than earlier generations do. Millennials want a career that is secure, and they want to be able to keep that career for a long time, but that career isn't necessarily spent with a single employer. Instead, millennials focus on constantly updating their skill set and keeping pace with the latest technology and trends in their career. With fine-tuned skills, millennials are able to move seamlessly from one job to another while maintaining a secure career. For millennials, a secure career is more important than a single secure job.

Perhaps this explains why workers in this generation enter the workforce expecting to work many jobs in their lifetime.

And, although staying at a job for only one or two years was frowned upon by members of older generations, millennials are willing to change jobs in a short time span if they find a more promising opportunity. This gives millennials the opportunity to experiment with different careers. They are willing to switch jobs as often as needed to find a job that is a better fit for them, or to find a job that offers better benefits, higher pay, or more flexibility, a luxury that had not been possible with previous generations.

But what's even more important to millennial employees is having a sense that they are making a difference. They are change makers who want to contribute something valuable to the organizations they work for. According to a 2016 Gallup Poll survey, "[Millennials] want their work to have meaning and purpose. They want to use their talents and strengths to do what they do best every day. They want to learn and develop. They want their job to fit their life."[4]

Millennials crave flexibility. Many prefer to have the option of working three or four days of a five-day week from a home office or coffee shop, where they feel they can get more work done. In fact, research has shown that employees are most engaged when they are able to spend 60 to 80 percent of their week working from home.[5] Millennials also value flexible scheduling, allowing them to fit other activities into their work day. As more

As of 2017, the average American worker retires at age 63.

millennials enter the workforce, it's likely that these workplace values will begin to shift the way Americans work.

BABY BOOMERS REACH RETIREMENT

On the other end of the workforce spectrum is the baby boomer generation, which is nearing the age of retirement. Nearly 25 percent of the workforce will be 55 years old or older by the year 2024.[6] But with people living longer lives—the average life expectancy in the United States increased by nine years between 1960 and 2011, jumping from 69.7 to 78.7 years—boomers are

RETIREMENT AGE ON A SLIDING SCALE

Although the official retirement age at which workers can begin to collect Social Security benefits has traditionally been 65 years, legislation passed in 1983 bumped that age up to 66 years for boomers born between 1943 and 1954. For those born in 1960 or later, the age of retirement will be 67 years.[8] The government offers a bonus for those who decide to delay collecting Social Security benefits. For each year a worker puts off collecting benefits after the age of 66 years, the amount collected increases by 8 percent. These amendments to the retirement age are an effort to delay a projected shortfall in the Social Security budget.

faced with the question of what to do with their time after retirement.[7]

Typically, baby boomers have held fewer jobs in their lifetime, choosing instead to stay with one company for most or all of their career. As baby boomers retire, the workforce is undergoing a generational shift. With this shift, the workers of younger generations are beginning to influence workplace cultures and practices. With many good years still ahead of them, those of retirement age are sometimes choosing to stay in the workplace. Some decide to cut down to part-time work and remain in their jobs for a few years longer. Others are changing jobs completely, looking for careers where they can do something for the greater good of society. Many retirees decide to volunteer their time at nonprofits and service organizations.

However, the Great Recession changed everything for many baby boomers. Even those who wanted to stay in the workforce longer almost had no choice because the recession laid off many baby boomers from their jobs and wiped away savings and opportunities to retire. Eventually, as time passed and the recession eased, many baby boomers went back to work to regain what they had lost and to help ensure that they had money for the future. Experts are calling it an "encore" career, and they believe it will become a popular trend in the next five years.[9]

THE APPEAL OF OLDER WORKERS IN THE WORKPLACE

There are distinct advantages to keeping older employees on the payroll. According to Paul Irving, chair of the Milken Institute for the Future of Aging, "Older people have so much to offer as workers, colleagues and mentors. It is in the business community's self-interest to recruit, train, promote and retain them."[10] Not only do older employees help maintain and promote key knowledge about company processes, those who are older than 65 years also receive Medicare, which reduces the cost of benefits for the employer.

RETRAINING FOR NEW JOBS

Retraining for new jobs promises to be a trend that will continue to grow in the future. The days of going to college and then embarking on one career for the rest of one's working life are over. Instead, workers can expect to undergo a cycle of training or schooling for a new career, working in that career for a few

years, and then moving on to something else. According to Pew Research Center, 87 percent of working Americans think job training will be needed in the future. As of 2016, "45 percent of employed adults report they have pursued extra training to maintain or improve their job skills in the past year."[11]

This training is often provided by the companies. Many companies pay for their employees to pursue additional licenses, degrees, or certificates. Companies are already shifting their focus to retrain and increase the skills of their employees. Dan Schawbel, a research director at Future Workplace, noted in late 2017 that "there are currently 6.2 million job openings in America that are unfilled, which is up from 5.6 million during the same time in 2016. Companies can't find the right workers, that have the right skills, at the right time, which has slowed growth in the economy. Employers will be investing more money into their training and development programs in 2018 in order to fill their skills gaps and reach their full capacity."[12]

THE RETURN OF HANDMADE

In the future, advancements in technology, AI, drones, and automated vehicles will inevitably lead to a decrease in the number of hours Americans will need to work—or they may alleviate the need to work at all. What will the growing numbers of idle workers choose to do with their time?

Communities that were economically and socially devastated when steel mills and other industries shut down in the late 1970s through 1990s are paving the way for a resurgence in the arts. The rise of a do-it-yourself movement has been in full swing since the early 2000s.[13] This revival of crafting roughly coincides with the souring of the economy in the years leading up to the Great Recession.

As part of this movement, makers around the country have joined together to create makerspaces. In Columbus, Ohio, there is the Columbus Idea Foundry. The Foundry, housed in an old shoe factory, is filled with machinery. Members pay a monthly fee to use the equipment to weld, make jewelry, or shape table legs on a lathe. This making space is also a

STORY OF A PLANT SHUTDOWN

Youngstown Sheet & Tube, a steel mill in Youngstown, Ohio, announced its decision to close its doors on September 19, 1977. With the closure, 50,000 people lost their jobs, and those losses have taken a huge toll on life in the community.[14] In the many households affected by the closure, worries of how to pay bills and put food on the table became commonplace. Cases of depression, spousal abuse, and suicide increased, affecting the mood and well-being of the entire town. Youngstown was not alone; many other communities suffered the loss of big industry from the late 1970s through the present day. John Russo, who teaches labor studies at Youngstown State University, made a connection between Youngstown and other communities around the country: "Youngstown's story is America's story, because it shows that when jobs go away, the cultural cohesion of a place is destroyed. The cultural breakdown matters even more than the economic breakdown."[15]

gathering space, where like-minded creative types gather to talk shop and get creative.

This is a dream come true for members, including Terry Griner, an engineer and steam engine hobbyist. At the thought of being able to devote all his time to making things at the foundry, Griner said, "If we had a society that said, 'We'll cover your essentials, you can work in the shop,' I think that would be utopia. That, to me, would be the best of all possible worlds."[16]

DISCUSSION STARTERS

- How might the qualities millennials bring to the workplace begin to shape the culture of work in the future?

- How might workers begin to prepare for the reality of having fewer opportunities to work in the future?

- What do you think will happen to the economy if people are working less?

SEVEN

CLASS AND THE
WORKFORCE

W hat may be ideal for some people might not be attainable for many others. Some people can't afford to have free time. One major effect of increased automation in the workplace has been the disappearance of the middle class in the United States.

As automation has done away with jobs, it has disproportionately targeted middle-class occupations, leading to a shrinking middle class. In the more than 40 years between 1971 and 2015, the percentage of the population considered middle class in the United States has dwindled from 61 percent to 50 percent.[1] In a Pew Research study, 203 of 229 US metro areas studied

People throughout the country have protested, calling for the government to raise the minimum wage.

Nearly 9 million people work in the trucking industry, including the 3.5 million drivers. These jobs are at risk of becoming obsolete due to automation.

showed a decrease in household incomes between 2000 and 2014.[2] This trend is expected to continue into the future.

A NATION BUILT ON A STRONG MIDDLE CLASS

Historically, the United States has been a country where anyone can move across class lines. People who were born in a poor household can grow up to be in the upper class. But this has become increasingly difficult to do. For generations, the average American enjoyed a higher standard of living than his or her parents. This is no longer a guarantee. In 2018, income inequality in America is higher than ever, with the middle class on the verge of disappearing altogether.

The economic forces that made it possible to climb into

the middle class by way of a working-class factory job have changed dramatically. In the climate of the prosperous manufacturing years that extended from the 1950s through the 1970s, working-class jobs on factory floors, in which American workers tended to be paid much more compared with those in the same jobs overseas, were plentiful. And workers didn't need a college education to obtain such work. As this work is disappearing, jobs that are replacing them pay less—sometimes much less. At the same time, those in higher-paying professional fields are making more.

As Mark Hamrick of Bankrate.com explained, "Income inequality, or the hollowing out of the middle class, has been seen in both the short-term and in the years going back before the financial crisis and the Great Recession. The loss, or migration, of manufacturing jobs is part of the story."[3]

HOUSING BUBBLE

One of the key contributing factors to the Great Recession was the bursting of the housing bubble. In the years before the stock market crashed, mortgage lenders granted loans to many families who couldn't afford to pay a mortgage. The brisk sale of homes drove up prices, inflating home values way above what they were actually worth. Many of these home buyers—lower-middle-class families with limited savings—defaulted on their mortgages. As a result, the average middle-class family lost 23 percent of its wealth from the beginning of the recession to the end.[4]

THE EFFECT OF THE RECESSION

In the wake of the economic downturn of the Great Recession of 2007–2008, companies looked for ways to cut costs. They accelerated plans already underway for plant automation, strengthened global supply chains to acquire deeper discounts on materials, and outsourced more jobs overseas, all at the expense of middle-class jobs.

Although those in the upper class took a hit when the economy dipped, they were able to lean on their assets and investments to weather the storm. And business executives

The recession hit businesses across the country hard.

In 2010, after the Great Recession, the median wage in Silicon Valley was $132,057. This came from tech jobs in companies like Apple, *pictured*.

reaped the rewards of cost-cutting measures with increased salaries. Those in the middle and lower income classes, however, may never fully recover. The reality is, the Great Recession significantly widened the disparity between those in the lower and upper classes.

THE RISE OF THE UPPER CLASS

Automation hasn't been the end of all jobs. Along with business executives, well-educated people who work in the tech industry have also benefited from automation. Between 2009 and 2010, in the aftermath of the Great Recession, wages stagnated throughout most of the country. But job opportunities for people with professional degrees in places such as New York City, New York; Washington, DC; and San Jose, California—finance and tech industry hubs—have

been abundant. During that same period, incomes grew by 11.9 percent in New York City and 8.7 percent in Silicon Valley, an area in California where many tech jobs are located.[5]

Although the Great Recession threw most of the nation into a tailspin from which it took years to recover, high-income earners have long since moved on. "The Labor Department predicts that tech jobs will grow faster . . . at a rate of 13 percent [in the 2010s]," according to *US News & World Report*.[6] The only struggle that the tech industry is facing currently is that it has more jobs than it has available workers. "As of 2016, the United States had roughly 3 million more STEM jobs than it had skilled workers to fill them," according to CNBC.[7]

MIDDLE-CLASS JOBS DISAPPEARING

Experts believe that the middle class is diminishing in America because jobs for this income group are disappearing— and fast. Economists predict "more than 60 percent of 173 occupations projected to decline through 2021 are middle-class jobs."[8] Furthermore, lower- and higher-class jobs are both predicted to increase. Economists can't say for sure what the future of the middle class in America will be, but they do know that technology will continue to play a role in the jobs of the future.

Affluent tech and financial areas are thriving, but unemployment rates are highest among people without higher education. Manufacturing jobs are continuing to struggle. According to technology news website TechCrunch, "In 1960,

Coal mining jobs, which were typically middle-class-worker jobs, declined from approximately 140,000 in 1990 to 50,000 in 2015, according to the *Atlantic*.

1 in 4 Americans had a job in manufacturing; today, it's fewer than 1 in 10."[9] In January 2017, the unemployment rate of people with only a high school diploma was 5.3 percent, whereas the rate for those with some college degree or an associate's degree was 3.8 percent. For those with a bachelor's degree or more, the unemployment rate was lowest, at 2.5 percent.[10]

The Great Recession had a significant effect on the workforce of America and continues to have an influence. In the future, jobs in technology will continue to be in high demand, whereas jobs in manufacturing will continue to diminish. This will further widen the inequality gap of Americans unless something is done.

DISCUSSION STARTERS

- Why do you think the upper class tends to add to its wealth in times of economic hardship?

- As an American consumer, what can you do to help the US economy?

- Do you think the middle class will ever disappear completely? Why or why not?

THE
FUTURE

Vast income disparities and huge differences in the opportunities for employment have pulled the upper and lower classes further apart as the middle class has begun to disappear. Yet automation and technological advances march on. If the United States is going to continue to compete on a global level, experts believe industry leaders need to further embrace these new advancements, innovate and expand on them, and begin to train all levels of the workforce for the jobs of the future.

EDUCATION

With the rapid speed at which technology is advancing, traditional workforce training may become out of date. In the

Steve Cousins, *left*, is the CEO of Savioke, a company that builds autonomous delivery robots, *right*. One of the robot's jobs is to deliver room service in hotels.

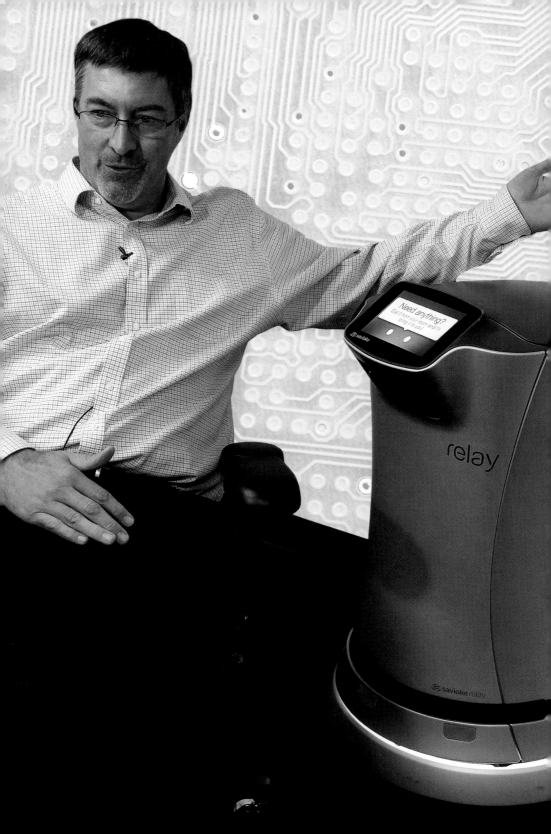

Some companies provide ongoing information technology training to help employees keep up with the latest technology.

future, additional training may be needed for the jobs that will be created. And many people agree. According to a 2016 Pew Research Center survey, "87 percent of workers believe it will be essential for them to get training and develop new job skills throughout their work life in order to keep up with changes in the work place."[1]

Tech giants such as Google are helping to pave the way for American workers to learn the skills they will need for the rapidly changing workforce of the future. On October 12, 2017, Google CEO Sundar Pichai announced a new program called Grow with Google, which commits $1 billion to nonprofits nationwide who are working to train American workers and build new businesses in the tech industry. In the launch letter for the program, Pichai explained, "We believe in leveling the playing field for everyone. The internet is one of the world's most powerful equalizers, and we see it as our job to make it available to as many people as possible."[2]

IN DENIAL?

Although there is significant data to support the fact that the United States is headed toward automation, some Americans don't believe that will actually happen. Approximately 32 percent of Americans don't believe the workforce will actually consist of robots and computers doing the work of humans. In fact, 7 percent of Americans firmly believe that it will definitely not happen.[3] And, although it feels like technology is taking over everything, most Americans feel their own professions won't be affected by the technological shift. They believe that their jobs will still exist in 50 years.

Google's CEO Sundar Pichai launched a program aimed at helping job growth in the United States.

Goodwill Industries will be awarded $10 million to help launch the Goodwill Digital Career Accelerator, designed to prep Americans for high-tech jobs. Grow with Google has a website that offers free training, tools, and events that walk students, teachers, workers, and entrepreneurs through the steps to increase their skills, expand career opportunities, or grow their businesses.

Grow with Google kicked off its first on-site training session in Indianapolis, Indiana, in early November 2017. The two-day workshop included 20 class sessions, one-on-one coaching for all skill levels, and hands-on demonstrations. Google selected Indianapolis as the first city to host a series of in-person workshops because the city ranks number 5 in the country in growth for careers in STEM, or science, technology, engineering, and math. Like many other US cities, Indianapolis has a middle-income skills gap and could benefit from such

A RETURN TO INNOVATION

Two professors at Columbia University, Edmund Phelps and Leo Tilman, believe that America needs to return to the culture of innovation on which it was founded. The prosperity of the American economy has always been based on exploration, experimentation, and the generation of new ideas. But innovation has been in a state of consistent decline since the 1990s. To spur on and revive innovation, Phelps and Tilman have proposed the creation of a First National Bank of Innovation, with the purpose of providing capital to promising and innovative start-ups. Investing in and supporting innovation not only creates jobs, it provides key learning opportunities, even if the project fails.

a program. And, the city has the capacity and leadership to foster the necessary partnerships between Google and community organizations to make the program effective. In its first year, Grow with Google plans to hold workshops in Louisville, Kentucky; Oklahoma City, Oklahoma; Savannah, Georgia; and other US cities.

INDUSTRIES OF THE FUTURE

So what are the industries of the future? Which industries can be expected to thrive?

The digital revolution, which began with the development of the internet and email in the 1990s, has advanced by leaps and bounds in the years since. Those advancements have changed the world in ways no one could have imagined. At the center of the digital revolution is the tech industry, which will continue to play a prominent role in the US and global economies in the years to come.

Tech jobs at the forefront of future advancements include software engineer, jobs developing internet infrastructure, and jobs in big data analytics, cybersecurity, and genomics. Big data analytics examines massive amounts of data to look for hidden patterns, connections, and other information. Having these capabilities enables companies and organizations to use the data to inform decisions, develop new products, and save money. Cybersecurity refers to the technology and processes used to protect networks, data, devices, and programs from attack or unauthorized access. And genomics is the science of researching and developing solutions to health problems using our own DNA.

The digital age is being powered in part by the developing renewable-energy industry. Through 2040, the US Energy Information Administration predicts that the fastest-growing power source will be renewable energy, including wind and solar.[4] According to a study by the US Department of Energy in 2017, 6.4 million Americans work in the energy industry, and 300,000 jobs were added in 2016.[5] The majority of these new jobs were in renewable energy. The fastest-growing jobs include wind turbine technician, solar installer, clean-car engineer, sustainable builder, and sustainability professional, someone who makes

As Americans continue to adapt to the ever-changing workforce, one thing is certain: they will have to get used to working with robots.

recommendations on how to make buildings more energy efficient.[6]

In addition, there is some hope for blue-collar workers to also continue to use their skills in the future. Although automation and robots will be a part of many careers in the years ahead, there will still be a need for someone to work in those jobs managing the automation. There will be a need for electricians, mechanics, maintenance workers, and welders to work on these robots and automated devices in the future. In fact, experts say these jobs are expected to increase—and pay well.

And, as technological advances continue to develop across multiple industries, there is no doubt that in 20, 40, or 60 years, the workforce will include jobs that don't exist today. There is simply no way to definitively predict what those jobs of the future might be. All we can know for sure is that the future of work in America is changing, and adaptation will be necessary to keep up.

DISCUSSION STARTERS

- What are three things today's students can do to prepare for a career in the future?

- What skills do you think will be important in America's future workforce?

- Do you think the gig economy will work for Americans? Why or why not?

ESSENTIAL FACTS

SIGNIFICANT EVENTS

- In the 1990s, work as Americans had known it changed significantly with the introduction of the internet to the general public. By using PCs connected to the internet, any information was just a click away. The internet also offered a new venue through which businesses could sell their products and services, which eventually had a negative effect on local, independently owned stores.

- In 2007, Apple introduced the iPhone, a smartphone that is essentially a handheld computer, which allowed users to make phone calls, take photos, listen to music, surf the internet, and check email. In later versions, users gained access to Siri, an automated personal assistant.

- The stock market crash and subsequent economic recession of 2008–2009 forced many companies to lay off workers and look for ways to cut costs. Manufacturers responded by outsourcing some jobs to overseas markets, where labor was less expensive, and by automating more jobs on the factory floor. These events accelerated the major shifts in the US economy that will shape the future of work.

- The founding of digital-platform companies such as Airbnb in 2008 paved the way for everyday people who have space to rent in their homes or apartments to join the growing gig economy. In the years since, Uber, Lyft, and other digital companies have provided the platform for entrepreneurs to make extra cash on a flexible schedule. This will be one form of making an income in the future.

KEY PLAYERS

- Uber employs many people in the gig economy who want to pick up part-time work and make their own hours.

- Airbnb offers people extra income through renting out their living space for money.

- Apple has created thousands of tech jobs across the country.

- Google has developed a program called Grow with Google that aims to provide additional technology training for employees.

- Etsy is an e-commerce website that allows people to sell products they create as part of their hobbies.

IMPACT ON SOCIETY

Technological advancements during the past 30 years have set in motion a shift from a manufacturing-based economy to a digital economy. This shift, ushered in by automation, AI, and other advances, has made many jobs, especially for the lower-middle class and working class, obsolete. In the future, there will be less work and more free time as more efficient, automated systems take over the work once done by humans.

QUOTE

"[Millennials] want their work to have meaning and purpose. They want to use their talents and strengths to do what they do best every day. They want to learn and develop. They want their job to fit their life."

—Gallup Poll

GLOSSARY

AGRARIAN SOCIETY
A community in which skilled craftspeople make all the goods, clothing, tools, and food needed and sell their wares at markets or exchange them through trade.

ARTIFICIAL INTELLIGENCE (AI)
The intelligence displayed by machines or computers.

AUTOMATION
The technology that enables tasks to be performed without human assistance.

AUTONOMOUS VEHICLES
Cars and trucks that are programmed to drive a certain course without a human driver.

DIGITAL PLATFORM
The website or other digital framework provided by companies such as Airbnb, Uber, and Lyft that allows contractors to provide services for the company.

GENOMICS
The science of studying a general DNA sequence to find cures for diseases and to develop drugs that fight genetic diseases.

GIG ECONOMY
An economy in which people complete a variety of tasks and jobs to earn their income.

GLOBALIZATION
The movement toward a world more connected by trade, finance, and communications.

GROSS NATIONAL PRODUCT (GNP)
The total value of the products and services produced in a country in a given period.

OUTSOURCING
The manufacturing practice of having certain production lines completed in countries overseas to save labor costs.

OVERSPECULATION
Business transactions that carry a lot of risk but promise big returns on investment if all goes according to plan.

SECURITY NET
The benefits typically offered by companies to their employees, including health-care benefits, disability insurance, and retirement plans.

SOCIAL SECURITY
A US program started in the 1930s to provide retirement income for people over the age of 65.

3-D PRINTING
A printing process in which material is added in layers, as directed by a computer program, to create a three-dimensional object.

ADDITIONAL
RESOURCES

SELECTED BIBLIOGRAPHY

Mulcahy, Diane. *The Gig Economy: The Complete Guide to Getting Better Work, Taking More Time Off, and Financing the Life You Want!* New York: AMACOM, 2017. Print.

Peck, Don. "Can the Middle Class Be Saved?" *The Atlantic*. The Atlantic Monthly Group, Sept. 2011. Web. 12 Oct. 2017.

Schwab, Klaus. *The Fourth Industrial Revolution*. New York: Penguin, 2017. Print.

FURTHER READINGS

Christen, Carol. *What Color Is Your Parachute? For Teens, Third Edition: Discover Yourself, Design Your Future, and Plan for Your Dream Job*. Berkeley, CA: Ten Speed Press, 2015. Print.

Cinnamon, Ian, and Romi Kadri. *DIY Drones for the Evil Genius: Design, Build, and Customize Your Own Drones*. New York: McGraw Hill, 2016. Print.

Hughes, Cameron. *Robot Programming: A Guide to Controlling Autonomous Robots*. Indianapolis, IN: Que Publishing, 2016. Print.

ONLINE RESOURCES

Booklinks
NONFICTION NETWORK
FREE! ONLINE NONFICTION RESOURCES

To learn more about the future of work in America, visit **abdobooklinks.com**. These links are routinely monitored and updated to provide the most current information available.

MORE INFORMATION

For more information on this subject, contact or visit the
following organizations:

COMPUTER HISTORY MUSEUM

1401 N. Shoreline Boulevard
Mountain View, CA 94043
650-810-1010
computerhistory.org

The exhibits at the Computer History Museum encompass the 40-plus
years computers have been part of everyday life. They include hardware,
photographs, video, memorabilia, and software documentation.

ROBOT REVOLUTION EXHIBIT

robotrevolution.com

This traveling exhibit explores what robots can contribute to our lives now and
in the future.

THE TECH MUSEUM OF INNOVATION

201 S. Market Street
San Jose, CA 95113
408-294-8324
thetech.org

This museum features exhibits showcasing technology used for
communication, exploration, innovation, and everyday life.

SOURCE NOTES

CHAPTER 1. THE FUTURE WORLD OF WORK

1. Derek Thompson. "A World Without Work." *The Atlantic*. The Atlantic Monthly Group, 2015. Web. 26 Sept. 2017.

2. Thompson, "A World Without Work."

3. Don Peck. "Can the Middle Class Be Saved?" *The Atlantic*. The Atlantic Monthly Group, 2011. Web. 12 Oct. 2017.

4. Tom Jackson. "The Flying Drones That Can Scan Packages Night and Day." *BBC News*. BBC, 27 Oct. 2017. Web. 3 Mar. 2018.

5. Christie Schneider. "10 Reasons Why AI-Powered Automated Customer Service Is the Future." *IBM*. IBM, 16 Oct. 2017. Web. 3 Mar. 2018.

CHAPTER 2. EARLY WORK IN THE UNITED STATES

1. "Working Conditions in Factories." *BBC*. BBC, n.d. Web. 24 Oct. 2017.

2. "Ford Motor Company Unveils the Model T." *History*. A&E Television Networks, LLC, 2009. Web. 24 Oct. 2017.

3. "Great Depression." *History*. A&E Television Networks, LLC, 2009. Web. 11 Oct. 2017.

4. "New Deal." *History*. A&E Television Networks, LLC, 2009. Web. 29 Sept. 2017.

5. Matt Egan. "2008: Worse than the Great Depression?" *CNN Money*. Cable News Network, 27 Aug. 2014. Web. 24 Oct. 2017.

6. Egan, "2008: Worse than the Great Depression?"

7. "New Deal." *History*.

8. "Unemployment Under Presidencies Since Depression." *New York Times*. New York Times, 9 Oct. 1982. Web. 5 Mar. 2018.

9. "GDP and Other Major NIPA Series, 1929–2012." *BEA*. Bureau of Economic Analysis, n.d. Web. 5 Mar. 2018.

10. "Baby Boomers." *History*. A&E Television Networks, LLC, 2009. Web. 24 Oct. 2017.

CHAPTER 3. TECHNOLOGY AND GLOBALIZATION

1. Tom Jackson. "The Flying Drones That Can Scan Packages Night and Day." *BBC*. BBC, 27 Oct. 2017. Web. 30 Oct. 2017.

2. Tom Risen. "Study: The US Internet Is Worth $966 Billion. *US News & World Report*. US News & World Report, 11 Dec. 2015. Web. 5 Mar. 2018.

3. "Two Million US Jobs. And Counting." *Apple*. Apple Inc., n.d. Web. 5 Mar. 2018.

4. Adam Davidson. "Making It In America." *The Atlantic*. The Atlantic Monthly Group, 2012. Web. 28 Sept. 2017.

5. Nick Statt. "America May Miss Out on the Next Industrial Revolution." *The Verge*. Vox Media Inc., 15 Mar. 2017. Web. 25 Oct. 2017.

CHAPTER 4. THE RISE OF THE SERVICE INDUSTRY

1. Reid Wilson. "Watch the US Transition From a Manufacturing Economy to a Service Economy, in One Gif." *Washington Post*. Washington Post, 3 Sept. 2014. Web. 27 Oct. 2017.

2. Andrew McAffe. "Manufacturing Jobs and the Rise of the Machines." *Harvard Business Review*. Harvard Business Publishing, 29 Jan. 2013. Web. 25 Oct. 2017.

3. Wilson, "Watch the US Transition From a Manufacturing Economy to a Service Economy, in One Gif."

4. Wilson, "Watch the US Transition From a Manufacturing Economy to a Service Economy, in One Gif."

5. "Home Health Aides and Personal Care Aides." *BLS*. US Bureau of Labor Statistics, 30 Jan. 2018. Web. 5 Mar. 2018.

6. "State Minimum Wages—2017 Minimum Wage by State." *National Conference of State Legislatures*. National Conference of State Legislatures, 2 Jan. 2018. Web. 12 Oct. 2017.

7. Julia Horowitz. "Here's Where the Minimum Wage Is Going Up in 2018." *CNN*. Cable News Network LLC, 29 Dec. 2017. Web. 5 Mar. 2018.

8. "Reports, Trends, and Statistics." *Trucking*. American Trucking Associations, n.d. Web. 5 Mar. 2018.

CHAPTER 5. THE GIG ECONOMY

1. Arun Sundararajan. *The Sharing Economy: The End of Employment and the Rise of Crowd-Based Capitalism*. Cambridge, MA: The MIT Press, 2016. Print. 10–11.

2. Derek Thompson. "A World Without Work." *The Atlantic*. The Atlantic Monthly Group, 2015. Web. 26 Sept. 2017.

3. Biz Carson. "How 3 Guys Turned Renting an Air Mattress in Their Apartment Into a $25 Billion Company." *Business Insider*. Business Insider Inc., 23 Feb. 2016. Web. 8 Nov. 2017.

4. Sundararajan, *The Sharing Economy: The End of Employment and the Rise of Crowd-Based Capitalism*, 106.

5. Sundararajan, *The Sharing Economy: The End of Employment and the Rise of Crowd-Based Capitalism*, 187.

6. Dan Kadlec. "This Is the Smartest Way for Millennials to Build Wealth." *Time*. Time Inc., 7 Jan. 2016. Web. 5 Mar. 2018.

7. Maija Unkuri. "Finland Considers Basic Income to Reform Welfare System." *BBC*. BBC, 20 Aug. 2015. Web. 1 Nov. 2017.

SOURCE NOTES
CONTINUED

CHAPTER 6. WORKFORCE TRENDS

1. "Millennial Careers: 2020 Vision." *ManpowerGroup*. ManpowerGroup, n.d. Web. 10 Oct. 2017.

2. Brianna Steinhilber. "7 Ways Millennials Are Changing the Workplace for the Better." *NBC News*. NBC Universal, 18 May 2017. Web. 10 Oct. 2017.

3. Larry Alton. "Why the Gig Economy Is the Best and Worst Development for Workers Under 30." *Forbes*. Forbes, 24 Jan. 2018. Web. 5 Mar. 2018.

4. Steinhilber, "7 Ways Millennials Are Changing the Workplace for the Better."

5. Steinhilber, "7 Ways Millennials Are Changing the Workplace for the Better."

6. Richard Eisenberg. "The Future of Work for People 50+ Will Surprise You." *Forbes*. Forbes, 22 May 2017. Web. 27 Sept. 2017.

7. "US Life Expectancy Ranks 26th in the World, OECD Report Shows." *Huffington Post*. Oath Inc., 21 Nov. 2013. Web. 2 Nov. 2017.

8. "What Is the Social Security Retirement Age?" *National Academy of Social Insurance*. National Academy of Social Insurance, n.d. Web. 2 Nov. 2017.

9. "Encore Career Choices: Purpose, Passion, and a Paycheck in a Tough Economy." *Encore*. MetLife Foundation, 2011. Web. 5 Mar. 2018.

10. Eisenberg, "The Future of Work for People 50+ Will Surprise You."

11. Anna Brown. "Key Findings About the American Workforce and the Changing Job Market." *Pew Research*. Pew Research Center, 6 Oct. 2016. Web. 5 Mar. 2018.

12. "5 Workplace Trends You'll See in 2018." *Workforce Institute*. Kronos, n.d. Web. 5 Mar. 2018.

13. Lauren Zumbach. "Growing Arts and Crafts Market Isn't Just for Kids." *Chicago Tribune*. Chicago Tribune, 29 Apr. 2016. Web. 5 Mar. 2018.

14. Derek Thompson. "A World Without Work." *The Atlantic*. The Atlantic Monthly Group, 2015. Web. 26 Sept. 2017.

15. Thompson, "A World Without Work."

16. Thompson, "A World Without Work."

CHAPTER 7. CLASS AND THE WORKFORCE

1. "America's Shrinking Middle Class: A Close Look at Changes Within Metropolitan Areas." *Pew Social Trends*. Pew Research Center, 11 May 2016. Web. 12 Oct. 2017.

2. Emily Badger and Christopher Ingraham. "The Middle Class Is Shrinking Just About Everywhere in America." *Washington Post*. Washington Post, 11 May 2016. Web. 12 Oct. 2017.

3. Quentin Fottrell. "The Middle-Class Paradox: Less than Half of Americans Say They're Middle Class." *MarketWatch*. MarketWatch, Inc., 24 May 2017. Web. 12 Oct. 2017.

4. Don Peck. "Can the Middle Class Be Saved?" *The Atlantic*. The Atlantic Monthly Group, 2011. Web. 12 Oct. 2017.

5. Peck, "Can the Middle Class Be Saved?"

6. "Best Technology Jobs." *US News & World Report*. US News & World Report, n.d. Web. 5 Mar. 2018.

7. Ruth Umoh. "The US Has a Shortage of Tech Workers. Here's How Kids and Schools Can Solve the Problem." *CNBC*. CNBC LLC, 23 Aug. 2017. Web. 5 Mar. 2018.

8. Martha C. White. "So Long, Middle Class: Middle Income Jobs Are Disappearing the Fastest." *NBC News*. NBC Universal, 5 Aug. 2016. Web. 2 Nov. 2017.

9. Abinash Tripathy. "The Future of American Jobs Lies with the Tech Industry." *TechCrunch*. Oath Tech Network, 27 Jan. 2017. Web. 5 Mar. 2018.

10. "Unemployment Rate 2.5 Percent for College Grads, 7.7 Percent for High School Dropouts, January 2017." *BLS*. US Bureau of Labor Statistics, 7 Feb. 2017. Web. 5 Mar. 2018.

CHAPTER 8. THE FUTURE

1. Lee Rainie. "The Future of Jobs and Jobs Training." *Pew Internet*. Pew Research Center, 3 May 2017. Web. 5 Mar. 2018.

2. "Grow with Google." *Google*. Google, LLC, n.d. Web. 3 Nov. 2017.

3. Aaron Smith. "Public Predictions for the Future of Workplace Automation." *Pew Internet*. Pew Research Center, 10 Mar. 2016. Web. 5 Mar. 2018.

4. Benjamin Hulac. "Strong Future Forecast for Renewable Energy." *Scientific American*. Scientific American, 27 Apr. 2015. Web. 4 Nov. 2017.

5. Daron Christopher. "5 of the Fastest Growing Jobs in Clean Energy." *RenewableEnergyWorld*. RenewableEnergyWorld.com, 10 May 2017. Web. 4 Nov. 2017.

6. Christopher, "5 of the Fastest Growing Jobs in Clean Energy."

INDEX

ABOUT THE
AUTHORS

DUCHESS HARRIS, JD, PHD

Professor Harris is the chair of the American Studies department at Macalester College and curator of the Duchess Harris Collection of ABDO books. She is the author and coauthor of recently released ABDO books including *Hidden Human Computers: The Black Women of NASA*, *Black Lives Matter*, and *Race and Policing*.

Before working with ABDO, she authored several other books on the topics of race, culture, and American history. She served as an associate editor for *Litigation News*, the American Bar Association Section of Litigation's quarterly flagship publication, and was the first editor in chief of *Law Raza*, an interactive online journal covering race and the law, published at William Mitchell College of Law. She has earned a PhD in American Studies from the University of Minnesota and a JD from William Mitchell College of Law.

KARI A. CORNELL

Kari A. Cornell is a freelance writer and editor who loves to read, garden, cook, run, and make clever crafts out of recycled materials. She is the author of *The Nitty Gritty Gardening Book: Fun Projects for All Seasons* and countless histories, cookbooks, and biographies for kids. She lives in Minneapolis, Minnesota, with her husband, two sons, and a crazy dog named EmmyLou.